FACE TO FACE WITH
WILD HORSES

by Yva Momatiuk
and John Eastcott

NATIONAL
GEOGRAPHIC
WASHINGTON, D.C.

FACE TO FACE

I have had horses on my mind ever since I was a girl, long before my husband John and I began to photograph them in the wild. I grew up in Warsaw, Poland's capital, after World War II. I saw ruined buildings, few cars, and many horses. The horses pulled wagons full of fresh vegetables, fruit, and milk from the farms—the food everyone needed.

The horses were strong but gentle, and I was not scared of them. I talked to them and touched their soft noses. They wore leather harnesses and worked

5

WHAT? HORSES WITH TOES?

■ Millions of years ago, small mammals called eohippus lived in North American forests. They had 4 toes on their forefeet and 3 on the hindfeet, with small hooves.

■ These plant eaters grew bigger. Certain toes lifted, so the horses could run and escape predators.

■ Over time, these animals evolved into larger ones, which we call equus. They walked on single toes with hooves, and some looked a bit like today's horses, zebras, and donkeys.

■ Equus evolved into modern horses. Walking across the land bridge from Alaska to Asia, they spread to Europe and Africa. They disappeared in North America, maybe killed for meat. Spanish explorers brought domestic horses back about 500 years ago.

hard. But in my dreams I saw them galloping with their manes flying, free as the wind. To me, they were the most beautiful animals in the world.

Many years later, I came to the United States and lived in Wyoming. One spring day, I drove to the Red Desert and followed a gravel road between flat-topped rocky hills called buttes. The snow had just melted. Then I saw a group of horses, standing very still and watching me. Their bodies were stocky, their winter hair long. And they had no brands, the identifying marks burned into the hides of many large ranch animals out West. Wild horses!

I grabbed my camera and walked toward them. The horses watched me curiously. It was a small family band with several mares, young foals, and a stallion with a mane flowing down to his chest. He sniffed the air, pawed the ground, and whinnied loudly. I felt he was warning me not to come closer.

I froze in my tracks, but it was too late. The stallion took off and galloped straight toward me. I turned to run, then tripped and fell on the ground. I heard his pounding hooves as he ran around me in circles, snorting and blowing. Terrified, I did not move. The stallion galloped away, gathered his

Protecting his band, a wild stallion circles me aggressively, hooves flashing. Making sure their families are safe keeps stallions busy, so they spend less time eating and sleeping than their mares.

family, and disappeared into the desert. My heart was beating hard, but I was happy. I had just met wild horses face to face. I also learned that instead of coming close and disturbing them, I must wait for the horses to approach me.

Later I introduced my husband John to the Red Desert and its wild inhabitants. Together, we searched for wild horses in remote mountains and deserts of the western states. And after spending years in the company of wild horses, we got to know them well.

MEET

Horses are the ultimate party animals. They love to groom, touch, sniff, play, and rest among their own.

THE WILD HORSE

Swift and sure, this stallion rushes across the Red Desert in a mock charge. He later veered off and galloped away.

Wild horses are sometimes called mustangs. The word brings to mind strength and courage, and comes from the Mexican-Spanish word *mestengo,* meaning "feral." But a wild horse is not really a feral horse. What is the difference?

Horses that used to live with people but no longer do are called feral. They escaped or were let loose by their owners. Such horses just trot down the road or jump a fence to join other horses. They hang around farms or buildings, seeking food and looking lost.

9

Protected by their warm coats of winter fur, a mare, whom we nicknamed Gimpy, and her newborn foal, Flag, endure another snowstorm in a clump of willows.

Wild, free-roaming horses know the rugged land they live on. They find their own food and water. They do not trust people. These horses are descendants of native wild horses that evolved on the American plains over a million years ago. They were later domesticated and brought back to this continent in the early 1500s by Spanish explorers. Some of the horses escaped and found freedom in the huge American grasslands. Surviving on their own, they soon became truly wild animals again.

Horses do not hunt, so evolution did not arm them with claws and wolf-like teeth. Their teeth are shaped to cut, chew, and grind plants. And like

This map shows how the wild horse (Equus caballus) began in North America and then spread through Asia and into Europe. They later died out in North America, but they were reintroduced starting in 1519. Today, isolated groups of wild horses can be found across the globe.

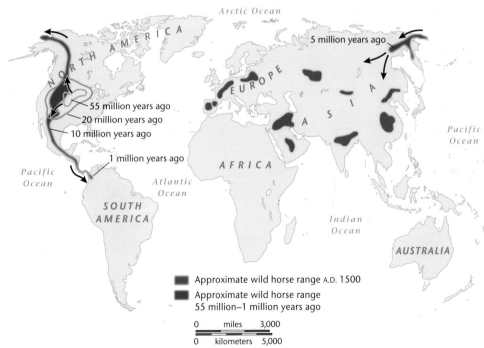

Arctic Ocean

NORTH AMERICA

EUROPE

ASIA

5 million years ago

55 million years ago
20 million years ago
10 million years ago

1 million years ago

Pacific Ocean

AFRICA

Atlantic Ocean

SOUTH AMERICA

Indian Ocean

Pacific Ocean

AUSTRALIA

■ Approximate wild horse range A.D. 1500
■ Approximate wild horse range 55 million–1 million years ago

0   miles   3,000
0   kilometers   5,000

HOW DO WILD HORSES TALK?

Horses say a lot with their bodies, but they also make sounds.

- **They neigh loudly when they look for other horses.**

- **They whinny softly by vibrating their vocal cords to say hello.**

- **They blow through their noses when they are curious or when they greet each other.**

- **They snort with heads high when they sense danger.**

- **They squeal or scream loudly when they are annoyed or fighting.**

other plant-eating animals, they are prey animals. They may be attacked and killed by predators.

This makes wild horses very alert. Always watching for danger, they may run away from people, a car—even a newspaper flying in the breeze. Their large eyes scan a lot of land, and their ears have many little muscles so they can swivel separately to catch sounds. Their strong legs carry them to safety.

Wild horses are smaller than domestic horses, and their long manes are tangled with burrs. They

← *Frightened by a distant helicopter, wild horses gallop toward a hidden trap set by government wranglers between sandstone buttes. Many of the horses will be released to run free again. Others will be moved to adoption centers.*

have heavy bones and hard hooves from running over rocky ground. Strong and athletic, they gallop, jump over obstacles, and swim across rivers.

Wild horses live in forests, mountains, deserts, grasslands, marshes, and barrier islands. They can adapt, surviving in many habitats. They tolerate the scorching heat of summer, as well as the deep snow and icy blasts of winter. Hordes of insects can make their lives miserable. They confront many dangers— avalanches, rock slides, lightning, and swollen rivers.

Play-fighting and dancing on their powerful hind legs, young stallions learn to compete. To get a mare when they are about five years old, they will fight for real.

FAMILY BANDS

Always close to his family, and warmed by the winter sun, Crow the stallion allows baby Flag to cuddle beneath his fuzzy chin.

One frosty spring morning in the Wyoming desert, we saw a newborn wild horse. Damp and shivering, the tiny foal struggled to stand. He tripped over his own wobbly legs.

The mare, his mother, licked and nudged the foal with her soft nose. He called, and she nickered gently. Soon he was up, nuzzling her belly. The foal drank the first warm gulp of her milk. He inhaled her smell. The mare sniffed his fragrant fur. These smells and sounds would help them recognize each other later.

↑ *Chased away from their families, young males join bachelor bands. "Bachelor" is a word that means "a male that does not have a mate." Plenty of grooming and touching helps them feel good again.*

We named the foal Flag because of his fluffy tail, and his mom Gimpy because of her slight limp.

Wild horses live in groups, called family, or harem, bands, almost all their lives. A band is made up of a leader, a dominant male horse called a stallion, his mares, and their foals. Wild horses usually do not like to be alone. But like other mares about to give birth, Gimpy left the band to have her baby and bond with her newborn. She knew that other mares sometimes try to steal new babies if they have lost their own.

After a few days of nursing and napping, Flag could already run. Since horses evolved on the plains, where they could easily be seen by predators, they are "runners." This means newborn foals have to get on their feet fast and run with the herd to escape danger.

We watched as Flag and Gimpy joined their band. The family greeted the newborn excitedly. Flag met the other foals. But when the big stallion came to sniff him, Flag started to clack his teeth like mad. Scared, he was saying, "I am just a little horse, please don't hurt me!" But the stallion, a black horse we called Crow, just wanted to protect him. So Flag slipped his head under the stallion's fuzzy neck and relaxed.

Soon the band moved on, and Flag followed. A few

weeks later, he started to skip around and play with the female foals, called fillies, and the male foals, called colts. When they strayed too far, Crow galloped after them, lowering his head. He snaked his muscular neck and herded them back to the safety of the herd.

Summer warmth came. Flag snoozed in the sun

while other horses grazed among beautiful desert flowers. The foals groomed each other's fur with their small teeth, which took care of their itchy skin.

Flag watched and learned from the young stallions. When they were about age three, they were chased away from their bands by older studs. They joined bachelor bands and had great fun galloping, kicking up dust, and chasing each other. Play-fighting on their hind legs, they bared their teeth and squealed. As they matured, they raided family bands to try to find a mate. During the breeding season of late spring and early summer, serious stud fights often broke out. Flag got out of their way so he wouldn't get kicked.

The summer heat increased, and water became scarce. Every evening, the lead mare would take the band to a waterhole. She ran ahead, and they followed. The stallion loped behind to protect them. Hot, dusty, and thirsty, they gulped the water down. They splashed and rolled in the sparkling pool.

The band soon moved on. Drinking places can be dangerous because predators often attack there. Except for mountain lions, few natural predators kill wild horses in the American West today. Still, they obeyed their instinctive fear and never stayed long.

MANAGING

← *Rounding up wild horses, usually with a helicopter and wranglers on horseback, helps control their growing herds on our public lands.*

THE HERD

← *Dusty and tired, captured wild horses crowd in a corner of a portable corral.*

If you fly low over the deserts of Nevada or the grassy peaks of Montana, you may see small groups of wild horses. Scattered across their home ranges—a valley or a group of mountains—these family bands form a herd.

These horse populations have to be controlled. To understand why, let's look back. After wild horses scattered around the continent, Native Americans learned to catch and ride them to hunt buffalo (or bison) and fight enemies. Later, thousands

➡ *A ranching family admires a cute wild foal they want to adopt.*

EAT, DRINK, EAT

Wild horses graze on coarse grasses and herbs dusted with dirt. This rough forage grinds down their teeth as they age, making it hard to graze. They grow weak and can't survive the drought and severe cold. Very few wild horses live to be 20 years old.

▬ Wild horses drink from springs, streams, and lakes. They will eat snow and break ice to get water.

▬ Besides grass, which they love, they chomp up to 6 pounds of leaves, wild flowers, thistles, and twigs daily.

▬ Starving wild horses may munch on tree bark, their dung piles, and even their own fur.

of wild horses were caught by "mustangers." They were sold to the U.S. Cavalry and to ranchers. But some were killed, and their meat used as pet food.

Then Velma B. Johnston, nicknamed Wild Horse Annie, told the public about the brutal capture and treatment of wild horses. Newspapers published stories about it, and school kids wrote thousands of letters. In 1971, the U.S. Congress passed the Wild Free-Roaming Horses and Burros Act. The

act protects wild horses as the living symbols of the pioneer spirit of the American West. It is now illegal to capture, harass, or kill wild horses.

Today, nearly 29,500 wild horses live on about 45,300 square miles (117,300 sq km) of public lands. They are free to roam, but their range is limited by fences protecting ranches, homes, industries, and highways. Wild horses have few natural predators. Left on their own, their numbers would nearly double

⬆ *Some captured wild stallions are trained by inmates in state prisons. The men must treat the horses gently in order to make friends.*

23

every five years. There would be too many horses, and they would graze their grassy range bare. They would run out of water and die of hunger and thirst.

The Bureau of Land Management, or BLM, is a government agency that manages the public lands. These lands have many uses. Wild horses share the range with grazing cattle, deer, elk, bighorn sheep, and pronghorn antelope. Companies want to use the natural resources, such as coal, oil, gas, uranium, and wind energy. Hunters, fishermen, hikers, and families camp and boat on the rivers and lakes.

To balance these needs and protect the range, BLM catches some wild horses. It also experiments with a special vaccine so the youngest mares will not bear foals for a few years. The captured horses are adopted or sold to people who can care for them. You may even know someone who has adopted, trained, and made friends with a wild horse.

By managing the herd, we help to preserve these wild creatures and protect their range, so that wild horses stay free and strong.

HOW YOU CAN HELP

⬇ *Stallions challenge each other by striking the ground with their front hooves.*

Wild horses lived near people for centuries. But we really began to value them after they were tamed for riding and for carrying and pulling loads. Today, some ranchers dislike wild horses, saying they compete with their animals for grazing lands. Some hunters and miners want to get rid of them.

Adopted horses have been illegally sold for meat. And wild horses are still shot and killed.

These horses are part of our wild open spaces. We love to see them running on the horizon or grazing peacefully. People come from all over to see them, photograph and paint them, or write poems and songs about them.

We value these horses and the tradition of their rich past. We like the way they make us feel when we watch them: free and strong. Just knowing they are out there enriches our lives. Here's how you can help protect wild horses.

▬The fate of all wildlife is in our hands. The laws protecting wild horses can change. In 2005, the government allowed the sale of these animals. Since then, many have been slaughtered for food or shipped to other countries for pet food. Hundreds more may be put to death. Ask your parents to help you write to your representatives in Congress, telling them you support strong laws to protect wild horses on public lands. Tell them you want the BLM to control horse populations by controlling the birth rate. A letter signed by you and your friends can help a lot.

▬Tell others about wild horses or write about them for a school report. Explain why we need to let them roam free in our grasslands, deserts, and mountains.

▬If your family has fenced pasture and loves horses, ask about adopting a wild horse.

▬Learn about the BLM's national fund to care for horses taken from the range because of fires or drought. Read about the Save the Mustangs Fund and the Mustang Heritage Foundation, both dedicated to helping horses.

IT'S YOUR TURN

Learning about wild horses may make you wish to watch them in the wild. Some BLM offices, guidebooks and Internet Web sites list good places to find them. Before you travel to hidden spots where the horses roam, practice observing wild animals right where you live.

Try to observe the wildlife in a nearby park. No feeding—that's cheating! Notice that all birds and squirrels have their comfort zone. If you come too close, they will move away. Discover the distance they need, and wait quietly. They may move closer and let you watch their behavior. Wild horses have their comfort zones, too.

How close can you get to domestic horses out in a big pasture? Observe how they fix their eyes on you, prick their ears, and move away together.

Try to be very patient. Sit down, be quiet, and avoid quick movements. Slowly, they may drift closer.

These exercises may help you watch their wild kin for a long time. But don't sneak behind rocks and bushes. Hidden shapes remind wild horses of predators, like the saber-toothed tigers their ancestors used to fear.

⬇ *A good roll on his back relieves a horse of insect bites and other itchy spots.*

FACTS AT A GLANCE

↓ *A good breakfast of rich mare's milk will help this tiny colt grow into a powerful stallion.*

▬ Scientific Name
Equus caballus

▬ Common Names
Wild horse, feral horse, and mustang.

▬ Size
Their height varies from about 58 inches (150 cm) to 62 inches (160 cm) tall, measured from the ground to the withers—the place where the neck meets the back. Adult wild horses weigh from 700 to 1,000 pounds (318 kg to 454 kg).

▬ Lifespan
Many wild horses live about 12-15 years. Few live to age 20.

▬ Special Features
Wild horses have developed strong leg bones, hard hooves, and great endurance through generations of living rough. And like all horses, they have the largest eyes of any land mammal. They can see almost entirely behind themselves without moving their heads. Their eyes are actually bifocals. The top half of the lens can focus on objects far away (such as predators) while the bottom half of the lens focuses on a blade of grass a few inches away. Each ear can swivel around independently, so they can accurately locate sounds. And horses can sleep comfortably standing up as well as lying down. That helps them get moving fast to escape danger day or night.

▬ Habitat
Horses live in the grasslands, foothills, and semi-desert (arid) regions of the West and in forest fringes and on sandy barrier islands in the eastern U.S. Wild horses are also found in similar places in South America, Africa, Asia, Australia, and New Zealand.

▬ Food
Wild horses eat grasses, low-growing plants, leaves, wild flowers, and twigs. They drink up to 10 gallons (38 liters) of water a day if they can get it.

▬ Social Habits
Horses like to stay close to

other horses. Wild bands number from 2 or 3 to more than 20 mares and their young. Herd animals prefer other animals. But they can get used to people and can even be trained. They will eventually accept their human family as their new herd.

Reproduction

Wild horses breed in the spring and early summer. Stallions begin mating with fillies when they are three or four years old. Pregnancy lasts 11 months, and then a single foal is born; twins are rare. Foals can stand up and walk soon after birth. They nurse for about two or three years, until just before the mother bears her next baby, but they also begin nibbling grass at about two months.

Population

There are about 30,000 wild horses living free on land in the West. Another 30,000 or so are kept in holding pens by the BLM. Several hundred wild horses roam barrier islands and forested areas in the East.

Biggest Threats

The wild horses in America have few natural enemies today. In the West, mountain lions sometimes attack horses. Wolves may someday be a menace too. But the biggest challenge wild horses face today is loss of the lands they live on. Horse populations can grow rapidly, competing for land against ranchers, mining and drilling industries, and people wanting to build

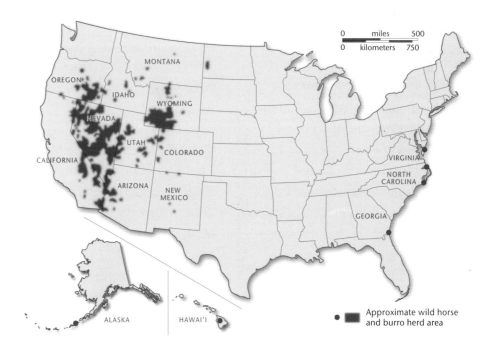

The map above shows where wild horses live in the United States today.

vacation homes. Adoption programs cannot save enough animals. But groups are working to protect wild horses. Our government is looking for a solution that is fair to horses and to people.

29

GLOSSARY

Bachelor: a male animal who does not have a mate.

Colt: an immature male horse four years or younger.

Domesticated: an animal whose ancestors were tamed and bred by humans to strengthen certain characteristics, such as size, shape, or temperament. Domesticated animals may be more delicate than their wild relatives.

Dominant: an assertive, often aggressive horse; the dominant horse can be either male or female.

Feral: a domesticated animal that has returned to the wild.

Filly: an immature female horse four years or younger.

Foal: a horse one year or younger.

Herd: a collection of family bands with home ranges that are close or overlapping.

Home range: the large area where a family band roams.

Mare: a mature female horse.

Predator: an animal that must kill other animals for food.

Prey: an animal, such as wild horses, that predators eat.

Stallion: a mature male horse.

Stud: a male horse that mates and produces foals.

Wrangler: a ranch hand; a cowboy

FIND OUT MORE

Books & Articles
Curtin, Sharon, Yva Momatiuk, and John Eastcott. *Mustang.* Bearsville, N.Y: Rufus Publications, 1996.

Hubert, Marie-Luce, and Jean-Louis Klein. *Mustangs.* Ontario, Canada: Firefly Books, 2007.

Hyde, Dayton O., Rita Summers, and Charles G. Summers. *All the Wild Horses.* Stillwater, MN: Voyageur, 2006.

Kirkpatrick, Jay F., and Michael H. Francis. *Into the Wind.* Minocqua, WI: NorthWord Press, 1994.

Roberts, Monty. *Shy Boy: The Horse That Came In From the Wild.* New York, N.Y.: HarperCollins, 2000.

Ryden, Hope. *Wild Horses I Have Known.* New York, NY: Clarion, 1999.

Ryden, Hope. *America's Last Wild Horses.* Guilford, CT: Lyons Press, 1999.

Skurzynski, Gloria, and Alane Ferguson. *Ghost Horses (Mysteries in Our National Parks).* Washington, D.C.: National Geographic Society, 2000.

Films
Touching Wild Horses. An award-winning film about a boy, his aunt, and a herd of wild horses. 2002.

The Silver Stallion. A mother's tale about wild horses in Australia comes to life for her daughter. Parents Choice Award. 2004.

Web Sites
http://www.blm.gov/wo/st/en/prog/wild_horse_and_burro.html.

http://www.ford.com/our-values/environment. Go to Nature and Wildlife and then Save the Mustangs.

www.wildhorsepreservation.org.

INDEX

Boldface *indicates illustrations.*

Adoptions 13, **22,** 25, 26

Bachelor bands **16,** 19, 29
Behavior
bachelor bands **16,** 19
 feeding **4,** 22
 fleeing from danger 12, **12–13**
 foals **14,** 15, 16–17, 19, **24–25**
 grooming **16,** 19
 mares 15, 19, **24–25**
 protecting family band 6–7, **7, 8,**
  16, 17, 19
 resting **17**
 social behavior **9,** 28–29
 stallions 6–7, **7, 8, 14, 15,**
  18–19, 19, **26**
Bureau of Land Management
 (BLM) 25, 26

Captured horses **20, 21, 23,** 25
Colts 17, 30
Communication 12
Crow (stallion) 16, 17

Diet 22, 28, **28**

Ears 12, 28
Eohippus 6
Equus 6, 28, 29
Evolution 6, 16
Eyesight 12, 28

Family bands 6, 16, 28–29
Feeding **4,** 22, 28, **28**
Feral horses 9, 11, 30
Fillies 17, 29, 30
Flag (foal) **10,** 15–17
Foals
 definition 30
 with mother **10, 24–25, 28**
 newborn 15, 16, 29
 with stallion **14**

Gimpy (mare) **10,** 15–16

Glossary 30
Grazing **4,** 22

Habitat 13, 28
Herds 21, 30
History 11, 21–22
Hooves 13
Horse meat 22, 26
How you can help 26

Johnston, Velma B. 22

Laws 22–23, 26
Lifespan 22, 28

Maps 11, 29
Mares
 definition 30
 with foal **10,** 15, **24–25, 28**
 grazing **4**
 reproduction 25, 29
 stealing newborn foals 16
Mustangs 9

Population 29
Predators 12, 19, 29
Public lands 23, 25

Reproduction 25, 26, 29

Size 28
Sleeping 28
Stallions
 cuddling foal **14**
 definition 30
 dominance **18–19**
 fighting **15,** 19, **26**
 mating 29
 protecting family band 6–7, **7,**
  8, 16, 17, 19

Teeth 11
Threats 26, 29
Toes 6

Water sources **18–19,** 19, 22
Wild horses
 definition 11
 history 11
Work horses 5–6

RESEARCH & PHOTOGRAPHIC NOTES

We have been following wild horses for many years. Before each trip we check our truck's tires and its engine, and inspect our hiking boots. We pack our equipment, sleeping gear, and plenty of food. The rugged and lonely places we go to have no repair garages or stores for miles and miles.

Finding wild horses may take us days. They are always on the move, looking around for grass and water. They look for shady and windy places to keep insects away in summer, and for windblown slopes with exposed forage in winter. When we spot them in a canyon or along a rocky ridge, we grab our equipment and split up. John and I move and photograph differently, and we don't want our horses getting spooked by the other person.

Like a mother carrying a toddler, John hikes with his big tripod, heavy Canon camera, and a long 600mm lens on his hip. He is ready to drop to one knee, swing the tripod into position, and photograph instantly. He packs other lenses, spare batteries and a walkie-talkie in his fanny pack, and wraps extra clothes around his waist. He often carries 40 to 50 pounds, but he never seems to complain.

I carry my camera with a 500mm lens at the ready, and stuff the rest of the gear in my backpack with some warm and windproof clothes I will need when the temperature drops. I also have my walkie-talkie. We are often hiking across crumbling and dangerous slopes, so if one of us sprains an ankle or breaks a leg, we can get in touch with the other person, who can help us back to our car or call for help.

THIS BOOK IS DEDICATED TO THE
WILD HORSES WE GET TO KNOW
AND LOVE. IT IS ALSO DEDICATED
TO OUR DAUGHTER TARA, WHO
LOVES ALL EQUINE BEINGS.
— YM & JE

Acknowledgments
We thank every wild horse who managed
to tolerate our presence, and understand
every horse who did not. In their eyes,
we must be just stubborn horseflies,
buzzing around without an invitation. We
are grateful to Wyoming's BLM officers
and wranglers, particularly Thor
Stephenson and Roy Packer, as well as
Vic McDarment, Bobby Anderson, Todd
Nunn, and Jim Williams. We learned
much from the late Reverend Floyd
Schwieger, who cared so well for the
Pryor Mountains mustangs, and from
Linda Coats-Markle, a wild horse special-
ist from Montana's BLM. Special thanks
go to the Brislawn family, owners of the
Cayuse Ranch in Wyoming, who let us
photograph and play with their wonder-
ful Spanish mustangs. We appreciate the
help of Dean Bolstad, Deputy Division
Chief of the BLM's Wild Horse and Burro
Program in Nevada. We are grateful to
Minden Pictures agency for providing
scans of many of the images. And we
thank Kel Van Demark, who has touched
our 4-wheel-drive vehicles with enough
magic to get us where we want to go.
—Yva Momatiuk and John Eastcott

The publisher gratefully acknowledges
the assistance of Christine Kiel, K-3
curriculum and reading consultant; the
American Museum of Natural History;
and Jay F. Kirkpatrick, PhD, Director,
the Science and Conservation Center.

Published by the
National Geographic Society

John M. Fahey, Jr., *President and*
  Chief Executive Officer

Gilbert M. Grosvenor,
  Chairman of the Board

Tim T. Kelly,
  President, Global Media Group

John Q. Griffin,
  President, Publishing

Nina D. Hoffman, *Executive Vice*
  President; President, Book
  Publishing Group

Staff for This Book

Nancy Laties Feresten, *Vice President,*
  Editor-in-Chief of Children's Books

Bea Jackson, *Design and Illustrations*
  Director, Children's Books

Amy Shields, *Executive Editor*

Jennifer Emmett, Mary Beth Oelkers-
  Keegan, *Project Editors*

David M. Seager, *Art Director*

Lori Epstein, *Illustrations Editor*

Jocelyn G. Lindsay, *Researcher*

Carl Mehler, *Director of Maps*

Felita Vereen-Mills, *Senior*
  Administrative Assistant

Jennifer Thornton, *Managing Editor*

Grace Hill, *Associate Managing Editor*

R. Gary Colbert, *Production Director*

Lewis R. Bassford, *Production Manager*

Rachel Faulise, Nicole Elliott,
  Manufacturing Managers

Susan Borke, *Legal and Business Affairs*

Book design by David M. Seager. The body
text of the book is set in ITC Century.
The display text is set in Knockout and
Party Noid.

Library of Congress
Cataloging-in-Publication Data

Momatiuk, Yva, 1940-
 Face to face with wild horses / by Yva
Momatiuk and John Eastcott.
    p. cm.
 Includes bibliographical references and
index.
ISBN 978-1-4263-0466-8 (hardcover : alk.
paper)
ISBN 978-1-4263-0467-5 (library binding :
alk. paper)
1. Wild horses—Juvenile literature. 2. Wild
horses—Pictorial works. 3. Photography of
horses—Juvenile literature. I. Eastcott,
John, 1952- II. Title.   SF360.M66 2009
599.665'5--dc22

Front cover Face to face with a mustang filly;
front flap: A young stallion in Pryor Mountain
Wild Horse Range, Montana. *Back cover:* A
band of horses in a Wyoming meadow; Yva
Momatiuk and John Eastcott.